AF225940

Who's the Boss?

by
L. J. Martin

A Manual for those Interested in Success
The Employee's Bible
An Essay on Winning

If you're not willing to work for it, don't complain
about not having it.

About the Author

L. J. Martin is the author of over 60 book length works and several screen plays, however prior to becoming a writer he was involved in numerous businesses...but his forte was always selling. He's also a photographer with credits on covers of national magazines and with his work sold online. He founded Wolfpack Publishing with an associate, to whom he later sold to. In a short time Wolfpack became America's fourth largest publisher of Westerns. In his last year in business, prior to his career as a writer, he sold over one hundred million dollars in product. His expertise was customer/client relations, and his simple straight-forward customer relation methods are set out herein. If your employees can read, they and your business will benefit from this manual. Since becoming a writer, he and his wife, an NYT bestselling author (who was also a sales person before becoming an author), have over twenty million books in print both domestically and internationally. By far the majority of those are authored by Kat, whose career L. J. was thrilled to assist if in a small way.

"Do the right thing, even when no one is looking. It's called integrity."

Why this Manual?

Do you think you could have far more sales in your business? Are your counter people properly trained? Do your customers return...hopefully time and time again? You could have the best widget, or hamburger, or lawn care in the world, but a thoughtless counter person, phone person, or even delivery person can ensure your customer will not return.

This is the most basic instructional manual, one that any counter person can understand, and even sophisticated sales people might need to be reminded of...the basics, that bring those customers back time and time again.

"No matter how educated, talented, rich or cool you believe you are, how you treat people ultimately tells all."

BUTTONWILLOW BOOKS
Educational & How-To Books

"I don't trust anyone who's nice to me but rude to the waiter. Because they would treat me the same way if I were in that position" – Muhammad Ali

Table of Contents

A smart person knows what to say. A wise person
knows whether to say it or not.

Who is the boss?

Let's see...is it the guy who owns the company? Is it the company president? Is it the department manager? Is it your immediate shift manager? Is it the guy or gal who signs your check?

You'll soon learn it's none of those.

And, right after that mysterious 'who,' it's you who are the most important cog in the business wheel.

This may come as a surprise to you, but YOU are the foundation of your company, and other than the customer, the most important screw or bolt which holds the whole bridge together.

A recent morning's example is typical of what's happening in the country.

The hotel dinning room opens at 6:00 AM, or so says the front desk.

What a surprise, no one in the dinning room; clanking coming from the kitchen. If I was truly in a hurry I would have wandered into the kitchen and shouted out, "is anyone awake?" But rather I found a booth, seated myself, and went to work on my laptop. After ten minutes I would have come to a slow boil (no morning coffee = grumpy), but I realized there was free coffee in the lobby, so I fetched a cup and was content until 6:15 when the lady showed up with an "I had some prep to do." Being an old-fashioned boy, I presume prep would be done BEFORE opening...which is why it's called, "prep." As I was in North Dakota when this happened, I was not shocked to receive a seemingly sincere apology from the lady. Had I been in California....

Later that day my wife witnessed the same waitress try to seat two different pairs of customers at the same table so she wouldn't have to open another section farther from the kitchen...one of those pairs, obviously having private matters to discuss, huffed away. Lost business, lost revenue, a business just that much closer to closing its doors and throwing two or three dozen folks out of jobs.

To show that I'm not merely a grumpy old fart, I'm happy to report that the following morning, same time, I wandered into the same booth, waited only one minute and while sliding out of my booth to go to the lobby to fetch my own coffee, a very pleasant young lady hurried out of the kitchen and made me feel very welcome. She was not only efficient but when another old fart wandered in and with mouth gaping and turned so far down his false teeth were about to tumble out over his receding chin, ordered a dry bagel and immediately asked very nastily if they charged extra for a pad of butter and a dollop of jelly, then unsatisfied that he hadn't ruined her morning, asked, "so I suppose you charge for the water?" To my utter surprise and satisfaction the young woman was pleasant no matter how much black paint he tried to pour in her bucket, killing him with kindness.

I later suggested to the restaurant manager that she get a raise.

What got me started on this particular rant?

I think America needs to get back to work, and to do it with the same attention to detail many, most who were successful, did while I was growing up. And all they need to do is to recognize who's the boss in a free enterprise society.

We hear and read a lot about the "deep state." The deep state is merely employees, mostly of the government, who, in order to be fired it would take an act of congress. They are so deeply entrenched in their jobs it would take a D8 Cat to dig them out.

They aren't free enterprise employees, or they likely could not get away with incompetence...and worse, downright insubordination. But we're concerned with the great majority of us who can be canned.

Why has America gotten away from common courtesy, particularly at counters? Have things been too easy for us? Has it been too easy to get another job if fired from the current one? Have parents, most families with both working, been too busy trying to make a living to pay enough attention to raising their own children to be polite, empathetic, and to believe in that most basic of good personal relationship lessons: Do unto others as ye would have them to unto you?

One of America's most well run states is Utah. My wife and I drive the length of Utah at least once a year on our way from Spring-Summer-Fall residence in Montana to Winter in Arizona Utah takes care of business, maybe it's the wonderful work ethic of the Mormons, but when you go into a gas station mini-market run by some formerly foreign gentleman and his wife and four kids, to your great surprise you'll find the restroom open and CLEAN. In California all restrooms in those establishments are strangely out of order. Convenience Market or Gas Station = Out Of Order Restroom. Which is probably just as well as the one out of ten thousand who might be admitted to one reputed be in working order find it to be filthy, and you'd be better off to climb in the half-full dumpster out back of the place to do your business. But I digress....

Attitude Is Everything!

On one of those recent drives south we stopped at a combination gas station mini-market, and in the market was one of those chain burger joints, or a small version thereof. I seldom waste the calories on fast food, but we were in a hurry, so I approached the counter, the single customer in the place. A young man, hefty in size (saying "rotund" is not politically correct), wandered out of the small kitchen area and approached the counter. His bill cap was not turned backward, to his credit, but was pulled so low over his eyes they couldn't be seen, only half his nose, his pursed lips, and both his chins. Even though I was in a hurry, I decided to have a little fun.

He approached the counter, eyes unseen, and took up a position across the counter from me, ...and said absolutely nothing. No "hello," no "welcome to WalMart," no "may I help you,"...nothing. Soooo, I said nothing. Having been a salesman most of my life (and a damn good one, I might add) I know the value of silence. Dead, penetrating, attention getting, eventually very irritating, silence.

Finally, when I refused to break the silence, he began to fidget, and eventually (I guess he was afraid I was either voice impaired or was about to pull a revolver and hold the place up) he raised his cap, stepped back, and eyeballed me, his gaze very suspicious. I managed to keep a straight face, even though I wanted to break out laughing, but rather I gave him as hard a look as I could muster.

Finally, he managed, "You want something?"

I couldn't help myself, "No, I just came in to stare at you over the counter and see how long it would take to try and discover if I was a customer."

That, as I might have suspected, was greeted with a, "Uh?"

So, I ordered. And watched very carefully to make sure he didn't do something obscene to the food. He did glance over his shoulder several times to make sure this obviously insane old man didn't vault the counter and execute a rear attack.

And now, almost every time I deal with a counter person, I notice how poorly trained most counter people (supposedly sales people) are in this free enterprise country of ours, and to decide to try and do my very small part to try and show them the error of their ways, and make them aware of who's the boss in this great country of ours, and why that concept, observed by past generations, has assisted in making her the great country she's become.

Let me suggest to you that success, no matter how small a success one incident might seem to you, is one of life's greatest pleasures. It's one of the things that makes getting up in the morning a pleasure rather than a chore; it's a precursor to mental and physical health, it's the essence of a happy existence. It makes work a pleasure.

So, let's investigate a few ways to accomplish that goal, and why we should.

Why should you, as a counter person or sales person, maybe making minimum wage, give a damn who the boss might be?

If you haven't surmised the answer to that simple question as of yet, the customer is the boss.

The customer is boss.

Most religions offer the simple solution to success. It's the golden rule. Treat others as you'd like to be treated yourself.

"Whether you think you can, or you think you can't--
you're right."
— Henry Ford

What Good Are Customers Anyway!

Please consider that all the money any business accumulates, or doesn't, comes from the customer. It doesn't matter if it's a good or service your selling, the customer is the boss, and if the customer is unhappy, and no longer shows up to buy your good or service, there will be no more money; no more counter person, no more shift manager, no more general manager, no more vice president, no more company president, nor board of directors nor chairman of the board. And that sad process all begins with you and your relationship with the customer.

As said in nearly the first sentence, you are the foundation of your company, and other than the customer, the most important screw or bolt that holds the whole bridge together. You are the bridge between that customer and a happy, successful, fulfilling relationship with the business by which you are employed. Your actions can strengthen or crater that bridge, and maybe your job and that of others.

And therein lies the reason that government is perverse. No matter how good, or how poor, the service offered, the check still arrives at the end of the month. It's the one instance in our economy where the customer is not the boss, at least now in the eyes of the service provider. It's far too far a reach to understand that his or her paycheck originates with the taxpayer. Not that there are not some excellent government employees, some with some personal pride in what they do, but by the nature of "no profit necessary," they are few and far between.

It's not only your company that depends upon you, but think of the suppliers who count on your company's business, on the other employees who depend upon your company for their jobs...for those weekly or monthly checks that pay their rent or house payment and keep their kids in shoes and lunch money. And the landlord who owns the building or buildings your company rents...and the chain goes on and on and on.

Suddenly, you should realize how important you are.

So, don't let them down, and more importantly, don't let yourself down. Sure, you might find another job, it's again relatively simple. But if your company fails, you've failed to a great extent, and, trust me, you don't want to get in the habit of failing. It's bad for both your mental and, believe it or not, physical health.

What can you do to help insure your company's health, and success?

Easy, remember that each and every customer is the boss. Is that any easy chore? Usually it is, however, many times it's not. As I pointed out in the introduction to this book, some customers are tougher than others. Some are downright obnoxious, and those are the ones who'll test your patience, your resolve to make sure your company is successful.

You must approach every customer with an open mind, you must have no preconceived notions about that man or woman across the counter. Don't judge. You don't know, for instance, that he or she was not informed that morning that they had terminal cancer. Would you be less than bubbly under that circumstance? His or her mother may have died that morning. Or even merely her cat or his dog (more important than mother to some in this perverted society we've created). Or it may simply be that they've run out of money and this hamburger you're selling may be the last meal they can afford until day after tomorrow when they get paid again.

Or they may be one of the very few human beings who's just a smartass or who believes that every glass is half empty rather than half full.

But you'll never know which customer is which, or why they have the attitude that makes you want to give them less than stellar service.

Your job, one you've chosen to take money to perform, is a trust. It's a trust given to you by your employer, and he, and a lot of others are depending upon you.

Prove yourself worthy

I've never had a book, booklet, pamphlet, or manual, whatever this turns out to be, that had so much material so easily accessed as this "who's the boss." All I have to do is walk into almost any business and I'm confronted with material.

Only yesterday, needing a haircut, I called my local beauty shop (boy do I miss barber shops) and made an appointment for 10:30 AM, the earliest she said I could get in. I showed up at 10:05 and the girl was alone in the shop, sitting behind the greeting counter, reading a magazine. I asked, hopefully, if I could get in early. "No," she said, "I have a ten o'clock." I glanced at the time, now 10:07. What she should have said is "I have a ten o'clock, and I try and wait ten minutes to give my customers a break, but if she's not here by 10:10, I'll be happy take you early and she can take your 10:30." I don't have a lot of hair and I'm a fifteen minute cut, at the most. And a customer who's late should expect to "lose their turn."

But she didn't say that, and tempted as I was, I didn't offer her a lesson in customer relations.

I will tell you that I'm never late. It's my belief that folk's time is important, and if you're habitually late, what your saying is "my time is more important than yours," or, otherwise, "I'm more important that you are." I find it offensive to be late, and only tolerate it in others for a short time.

I walked across the street to grab some breakfast, as I had yet to do so. I rise really early, coffee it up, and usually try and have brunch so I limit the intake to two meals a day.

My morning continued to be more material for "who's the boss."

The cafe was fairly busy, two waitresses for about twenty people. It's a great breakfast for $5.00, two eggs, bacon or sausage, spuds, and toast, as their intent is to draw in customers for the casino in the next room. I climbed up to the counter and ordered, asking if I could get quick service as I had to be out of there in 25 minutes. To the girls credit she said, "maybe, but we're really busy." However, as she was honest, I said, "great, coffee to start." I waited for a few minutes, and counted, as she picked up the coffee pot and filled those already served four separate times, passing my upturned cup each time. I was six feet from the coffee pot, with an upturned cup waiting, shouting out silently for attention. I finally walked into the casino section (in Montana half the bars and restaurants have casinos) and offer free coffee while you pump your quarters into the machine. I filled up my own and returned to the counter.

To their credit, I was served quickly. I immediately pulled out my credit card and said "I'd like to pay." Which was ignored. I was also three feet from the register. Another waitress worked the register and I asked her, "May I pay," and she replied, "I'll get your server." As all I had was a twenty-dollar bill, I quickly asked, as she had the register open, "May I have change?" To which she replied, "You bet, in a moment," but closed the register and walked away.

I sensed a miffed waitress who was not about to help another waitress...to the distress of her customer, to the distress of her company, and to be factual, to her own distress but she was not smart enough to know it. No, she was not my waitress, however any customer in the house is the customer of each and every employee, and if that customer is given reason not to return, then all suffer.

I finished my breakfast and caught my "server," a term I was beginning to believe a misnomer, and asked, "May I pay." She said, "you bet," and informed me it was "three bucks...opp's, five bucks including the coffee." She then looked down her nose at me as if I'd committed a crime by going next door and filling my own coffee cup.

She didn't mention that the coffee was free in the next room, and she had no idea that I hadn't come into the restaurant from the casino in the first instance. I made no complaint, however, I made no something else as well, that something else was a tip.

That was the first time in twenty years that I have not left a tip. It's been my rule to tip ten percent for lousy service, fifteen percent for average service, and twenty percent for good service. Upon rare occasion for excellent service, over and above, I've tipped more. It doesn't have to be excellent service to get twenty percent, just good service. I figure the Good Lord has been good to me, and I like to pass a little along. But not yesterday.

And the young lady in the hair salon did not get off to the best second-start, as I entered at exactly 10:30, my appointment time, she was talking on the phone, obviously a personal call. She'd already demonstrated that her magazine was more important than her customer, now she was making sure I knew that her phone call was more important.

A person who realized who the boss was would have terminated the call when she saw me coming, which was easy as there's glass all across the front of the salon, and I'd seen her see me before I reached the door. Nope, four or five sentences later, she said, "I've got to go," with a tone that indicated she had to take care of a pesky customer.

I would have waited another three or four sentences before I excused myself without a tip of the hat, and most certainly without a tip, but she terminated the call.

I did redeem myself with the hair stylist (who's ten o'clock never showed, by the way) and tipped her (fifteen percent) as she gave me an excellent haircut, if not intelligent service.

I've since gone back to the same place, but made sure I had another operator and my next not only gave a great haircut, but excellent service, and got a 25% tip.

The crux of this article is your customer owes you nothing, he owes your business nothing, unless you're unique in what you offer, he can easily go elsewhere

Nothing!

You owe him/her everything.

You would not receive a paycheck were it not for your customer. Your company's landlord, suppliers, vendors, and others who depend upon some payment from your company/business, would not be paid, and consequently their suppliers, etc., and employees, would not be paid, were it not for your customer.

The customer is the boss; a truism, ultimate, final, without question.

If you're wise, you'll not expect to be given the benefit of the doubt by your customer, and you'll always extend that courtesy to him

He, after all, is the boss.

Self-Worth Begins With Honesty!

When I was six I was in what was then called a five and dime store. Probably the closest equivalent now would be the dollar store. I helped myself to an eraser. On returning to the car, my mother spotted the eraser in my hand. She promptly led me back into the store and had me not only return the eraser to the proprietor, but apologize, then to my great dismay, asked the gentleman behind the counter if he had a broom. He did, and she handed it to me and said "sweep the floor. I'll be back to check on you." With the proprietor exclaiming that sweeping was not necessary, he was promptly and decisively corrected by my mother, and I spent a couple of hours learning the error of my way.

Too bad today's mothers are not so astute, and today's businesses are not so fearful of being sued that they'd never let a six year old work in their aisle.

It was however a lesson long remembered.

When you work for someone, who benefits most from your being an absolute honest employee?

Were you to take an ice cream cone from a successful mini-market where you worked, would it break the place? Of course not. If you took a box of pencils or file folders home from the office for your personal use, would it break the lawyers or doctors for whom you work. Of course not.

So what's the harm of a little dishonesty?

You by now know how I like adages and proverbs. The one most applicable here is an age old one: the rotten apple spoils the barrel. When other employees see you habitually come in late (stealing time is stealing money), or taking extra time at your coffee break, or taking a book into the restroom and spending thirty minutes doing what should take five, then you are the rotten apple in the barrel.

But more importantly than your actions are as an influence on others, it's the lesson you're teaching yourself.

Getting away with something illegal, immoral, dishonest becomes a habit that will eventually crush the sprit and the soul. Some have said it far better:

"Whoever is careless with the truth in small matters cannot be trusted with important matters" -- Albert Einstein

"Honesty is the first chapter of the book of wisdom."
--Thomas Jefferson

"Living a lie will reduce you to one." –Ashly Lorenzana

"No legacy is so rich as honesty." –William Shakespeare

Many think that patience is a sign of weakness. It's anger that's a sign of weakness. Patience is a sign of strength.

Make It Easy On The Customer!

California seems to be the end of the earth when it comes to customer service...and most service employees might as well jump off the edge for all the good they are.

A simple question: Do you think you're more important to your place of employment than are your customers?

If you do, you're dead wrong.

I took an early ride with my cameras down to the harbor to take some pictures of the pelicans, which were working a bait spawn and from sixty feet in the air, doing their dive bomber act. As the morning drew on I drove to a small 20 seat café near the end of the harbor drive, one I'd read a recent review about in the local paper.

It opened at 7:00 AM and I was a few minutes early. There was only one car in the lot, and it was parked several parking spaces away, but I noticed a man behind the counter working, and he noticed me standing at the door.

Were I that man, whom I later found to be the manager or owner, with one customer standing outside, I would have opened five minutes early, if for no other reason than to allow my customer in out of the cold ocean breeze...and more so to make him feel welcome and even more so to make sure he didn't walk away. He did not come to the door, and even though there was another café a half-mile away and on my way home, I waited. At 7:00 he opened and had the coffee ready. I ordered, and before my order was up, a nice looking young lady came in, walked behind the counter, and put on an apron. Obviously she was a waitress. I had ordered, so I wasn't particularly offended that she didn't bother to greet me or come over to see if I needed anything.

I had parked in a place closest to the walkway to the café, in a lot with one hundred parking places. I would guess the parking lot seldom fills, however, the young lady parked next to me, nearest the walkway.

Why's that of interest?

Because the next few cars might have filled at least that first row, and then the next customer might have been handicapped or wearing a cast from his trip to the ski hill, and because he had an extra forty feet to walk, might have gone to the café down the road, where the employees were smart enough to park in the spaces far from the entrance, and leave the near spaces to the "boss," the customer.

As a young man I was impressed by a story on I read about an executive who'd just taken over Avis, then the number two car rental company in the country.

His executives, on the second day of his taking over, were surprised to arrive at the office and find their names had been painted out, removed from the curb that formerly fronted their "private" spaces.

Fearing they'd been fired, each of them inquired of him "why?"

He replied, "Did you notice my car was near the front door? If so, you should note it was because I was the first one in the office this morning. If you want a place near the door, beat the rest of the employees to work."

I love that story. A great manager is one who leads by example. To quote an old adage, "It ain't what you say, it's what you do."

What is anger? It's a punishment we give ourselves for someone else's mistake.

Let A Smile Be Your Umbrella!

Do you enjoy being smiled at? Isn't a smile actually a symbol of approval? Do you enjoy being approved?

I've often heard that it takes more muscles to frown than it does to smile. Research tells me that's not necessarily so. It ain't necessarily so, to quote another line from a song, as is the title to this section. So you don't smile just because it's easier. You smile because it's way, way better than a frown for your business, and consequently for your job, and believe it or not, for your health.

A smile protects your job, just as an umbrella protects you from getting wet.

You're not getting a smile from the customer, so why bother to give him one? Do you remember that customer who just found out he had terminal cancer? Do you think a smile is too much to offer him, even if the corners of his mouth are turned sharply down?

Want to know something else?

A smile is good for YOU, not only for the person who's seeing you smile.

Guess what? For a long while scientists have known that emotions are reflected by changes in the body. If you're happy, you smile. And guess what, it works both ways. If you smile, you get more and more happy. Do you want to be happy? If you don't, you need some help that I can't give you in this book.

Smiling to make yourself happy was first called the "facial feedback hypothesis." So let's give it a try.

Smile. I mean it, smile right now.

Sometimes the conscious effort of making yourself smile actually amuses you, and not only do you smile, but you giggle, if you're prone to giggling. I flat out guarantee you that if you smiled when I suggested it, you not only felt happier, but you'll enjoy this book far more. That's the emotional effect of the physical act of smiling.

There were actually experiments conducted to demonstrate the psychology of the smile. In the late 80's researchers had subjects hold a pencil in their mouths in different ways while judging cartoons, telling the subjects the test was about emotion, when in fact it was about the effect of flexing certain facial muscles upon emotion. Those who held the pencil crossways, making the face use the same muscles as used in a smile, judged the cartoons much more funny than those instructed to hold the pencil in other ways.

In a later study subjects were told to judge printed images, while "lifting their cheeks" which forced them to use the smile muscles, or to "furrow their brow" which forced the use of the frown muscles. The "lift your cheeks" group found the images much more pleasant that the "furrow your brow" subjects.

It's no surprise to me.

Smile and the world smiles with you, frown and you're likely to frown alone.

We all love to smile, and your customers love to see you smile, and will be happier, and will likely judge what you're selling them, be it donuts or Duisenberg's, much more pleasant.

"Any fool can know. The point is to understand."
– Albert Einstein

So, What Do You Want To Be?

I ask the question because it's important. What do you want to be, who do you want to be. It's important to your company, and sure as heck should be important to you.

The fact is you control who and what you want to be, and it all starts with attitude, and attitude is partially controlled by that simple act of smiling. And beyond that, attitude is most-certainly controlled by self-satisfaction, which is, or should be, the realization that you're doing a good job...a great job...and your hard work is appreciated. Another old adage, the last one: You can satisfy some of the people all of the time, and all of the people some of the time, but you can't satisfy all of the people all of the time.

But you can satisfy yourself that you're doing your very best to do so.

And you should, if success is your goal.

In closing let me quote a gentleman who came from Russia as a teenager, destitute, and became the owner and operator of one of the country's largest cattle, sheep and meat packing operations.

Oscar Rudnick was fond of saying, "The customer is not always right, the customer is not always wrong...but the customer is always the customer."

I don't know how it could be better said. Unless as by the fella who founded the world's largest chain of general stores...WalMart:

"There is only one boss. The customer. And he can fire everybody in the company from the chairman on down, simply by spending his money somewhere else." – Sam Walton

Join me for more at:

http://www.ljmartin.com

"Complaining about a problem without posing a solution is called whining." – Teddy Roosevelt

About the Author

L. J. Martin is the author of over 60 book length works and several screen plays, however prior to becoming a writer he was involved in numerous businesses…but his forte was always selling. His last year as a real estate broker he accomplished over one hundred million in real estate transactions. He's also a photographer with credits on covers of national magazines and with his work sold online. He founded Wolfpack Publishing with an associate, to whom he later sold to. In a short time Wolfpack became America's fourth largest publisher of Westerns. In his last year in business, prior to his career as a writer, he sold over one hundred million dollars in product. His expertise was customer/client relations, and his simple straight-forward customer relation methods are set out herein. If your employees can read, they and your business will benefit from this manual. Since becoming a writer, he and his wife, an NYT bestselling author (who was also a sales person before becoming an author), have over twenty million books in print both domestically and internationally. By far the majority of those are authored by Kat, whose career L. J. was thrilled to assist if in a small way.

"A pessimist sees the difficulty in every opportunity;
an optimist sees the opportunity in every difficulty.
--Winston Churchill

L. J. Martin Book List

Westerns:

Against the 7th Flag
Blackjack Brannigan
Blood Mountain
Buckshot
Condor Canyon
El Lazo
Eye for Eye
McCreed's Law
McKeag's Mountain
Mojave Showdown
Mr. Pettigrew
Nemesis
O' Rourke's Revenge
Revenge of the Damned
Rugged Trails
Shadow of the Grizzly
Shadows of Nemesis
Stranahan
The Benicia Belle
The Devil's Bounty
Tin Angel (Western Romance Written With Kat Martin)
Two Thousand Grueling Miles
West of the War

Wolf Mountain

Historicals:

Rush to Destiny
Shadow of the Mast

Action-Adventure, Crime & Thrillers:

Bullet Blues
Crimson Hit
G5 Gee Whiz (The Repairman No. 2)
Judge Jury Desert Fury (The Repairman No. 5)
Manhunter Series
No Good Deed (The Repairman No. 4)
Overflow (The Repairman No. 8)
Quiet Ops
Target Shy and Sexy (The Repairman No. 6)
The Bakken (The Repairman No. 3)
The Blue Pearl (The Repairman No. 10)
The K Factor (The Repairman No. 9)
The Repairman (The Repairman No. 1)
Venom
Who's on Top (The Repairman No. 7)

Contemporary:

Blood Lines
Unchained

Windfall

Non-Fiction:

Against the Grain
California Cocina
Cooking Wild & Wonderful
Cornucopia: Building A Greenhouse
Killing Cancer
The Write Stuff
Write Compelling Fiction (with Craig Martell)

Anthologies:

Paul Bishop Presents: Tales of Murder & Mayhem
The American West
The Trading Post
The Traditional West
The Manhunter Series
Western Fiction 10 Pack
Wolfpack Publishing Western Boxed Set
The Clint Ryan Series

Short Stories & Short Story Collections:

Holy Hell
Second is the First Loser
Short Story Collection & More

Slopes of the Sierra
Small Crimes
To Ride a Tall Horse
Western Short Story Showcase

"You will never reach your destination if you stop
and throw stones at every dog that barks."
--Winston Churchill